Yutori

Embrace the stillness

Priyanka

Made with ❤ on the BookLeaf Publishing Platform
www.bookleafpub.in
www.bookleafpub.com

Dedication

To those who long for stillness in a rushing
world,

who seek solace in the quiet moments,

and find beauty in the unnoticed corners of
life,

this is for you.

May these words be a gentle reminder

to pause, breathe and savour your life,

for in the spaces between, life truly unfolds.

Acknowledgements

Thank you for taking this journey with me. May this collection be a small oasis in your busy world, a reminder to breathe deeply and live fully.

To all those who have shaped me, inspired me and reminded me of the importance of slowing down, Thank You.

To those who unknowingly walked through the landscapes of my thoughts, Thank You for your contribution.

I submit this poem to the readers, whose thirst for art made this possible.

Preface

Yutori, a Japanese word meaning 'a sense of spaciousness' or 'room to breathe', captures the essence of what these poems hope to offer: a pause in your day to reflect, savour and slow down. These poems are written as an invitation to embrace the beauty of simply being and to savour all emotions, not just happiness.

Each page is a gentle nudge to stop and immerse yourself in the present. In a world where everyone rushes past, slow down and embrace the stillness, space and make time to notice the little things.

Away

Take me away, cried the weary mayfly,
From the scorching sun that pierces the air,
And rule every Summer with none to spare.

Take me away, cried the mayfly again,
From the crispy Autumn wind that blows all
around,
And the falling leaves that shall keep me
bound.

Take me away, squealed the little mayfly,
From the bone-chilling Winter that later sets
in,
And the ever-falling snow that shall keep me
threatened.

Take me away, sighed the mayfly,
Alas!,
From the Spring bugs and bees that are now
everywhere,

And the huge moths and worms that declare
warfare!

Thus spent the mayfly his entire existence of a
day,
Complaining and never appreciating this
boon of life,
Sigh!,
That passed by in the blink of an eye.

Biblichor

I ran my fingers along the mighty old books,
Enchanted, contented, trapped in my
thoughts,
For the warm fragrance from those delicate
pages,
Were flavoured with stories, adventures,
memories and more.

Transported was I, in each breath that I took,
To lands, eras and lives unknown,
For the yellow pages had an epic to tell,
With the rusty smell of the old folklore that it
held.

I sat there ignorant of the passage of time,
As if in a trance, trapped among the words,
For those paperbacks held the unique power,
To dissolve ones' guards and be lost in ones'
mind.

Each breath seemed as though the books were
breathing,

Each touch felt as though the books brushed
past,
For now was I one with the entire clan of
pages,
Awaiting an eager eye to reveal my tales.

Collywobbles

What gives you collywobbles?,
Asked the curious young man to the
time-worn lady,
Who sat beneath the cherry blossom beside
the lake,
With glistening eyes staring into the bliss,
gladly,
And a smile so warm it made you awake.

The delicate touch of the golden sunshine,
That wakes the slumbering leaves at dawn,
Like a warm caress that gives them the sign,
To leave the night behind, all troubles now
gone.
These give me collywobbles...

The first kiss from a young butterfly,

To the gay flower that bloomed overnight,
Both swaying in the wind nearby,
Drinking the nectar of love at first sight.
These give me collywobbles...

The first flight of the petite chick,
That was nestled safely in a branch up high,
With wings so tiny and a jump so quick,
Fluttering up slowly with the mother close by.
These give me collywobbles...

The loving smile from the eager child,
Who comes to play with the squirrels and
birds,
Whose eyes light up at the reassurance that I
smiled,
And chats away to all beings in her own
words.
These give me collywobbles...

The comforting touch from a loved one,
On a day so blue that the mind goes numb,
A touch that contains all words ever said and
done,

A touch that forever remains on the soul
therefrom.
These give me collywobbles...

This said, she gave him a flower,
To the young man who seemed to be glum,
Surprised and happy, he looked teary-eyed at
the flower,
He knew he would remember this in the days
to come.
The day he felt collywobbles...

Dream

Across the meadows and past the gurgling
brooke,
Ran I along with the breeze,
With daisies in hand that I eagerly took,
And the grass brushing past my knees.

Each breath took in the warm, woody air,
That was entwined with the floral fragrance,
With blood throbbing in the veins and pollen
in my hair,
It felt great, this adrenaline radiance.

As I slowed down above the green hill,
Saw I a clearing among the trees,
Where the sunlight crept in through the
branches so still,
And shone below on the dandelions and bees.

Among the trees were a tiny little fawn,
That played merrily with the bunnies around,
This felt surreal, with all worries gone,
And nothing but the gift of life all around.

With a cuddle and pat to the tiny beings,
Sat I gazing at the world in front,
It gave an energy that suppressed all bad
feelings,
Yes, I could be whatever or do any stunt.

Rushing past the hill I took a dive,
With nothing to fear, I spread my wings with
a scream,
That's when it dawned and my senses came
alive,
'Twas all but a fantastic dream!

It's been years now since that day I woke up,
Never since did I see a dream so vivid,
I yearn for that day now as I sit here with the
windows rolled up,
When I spot a few daisies that are pretty, I
must admit.

I gather them in hand and look up to see,
The tiny fawn that had been in my dream,
I follow her past the same meadow and the
bees,
Was it all really just a dream?

Euphoria

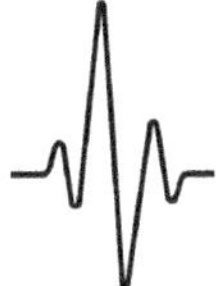

Amidst the chaos stood I with a silent heart,
Time seemed to freeze when the mighty
lightning struck,
Among the tide of people, when the rumbling
of the clouds did start,
I felt my whole being go numb when that
lightning struck.

There was no more the screaming of the
crowd,
There was no more the agony of mortals,
There was no more that feeling of being
bound,
There were no more strong distinct borders.

Realisation hit hard like a zealous wave,
And bursting was I in the ecstasy of the
moment,

That's when I knew my entire existence was
naive,
And this here, indeed, was a good omen.

I am me, you and everyone at sight,
I am the beautiful nature that is here,
I am the stars that twinkle at night,
I am the planets that you see far and near.

Afraid are men at the slight shadow of death,
Which comes to take you to your true self,
Little do they know that scarier is birth,
Where you are trapped in a dream with a
body of yourself.

This is the secret of life that you search,
This is a feeling that no wine can present,
This is where there's no mind, body or soul, o
dear!
This is where everything is pleasant.

This is Euphoria!

Feelings of the week

Monday marked the start of a glum week,
With the cold breeze setting the drowsy day
more weak,
The sun crept up as slow as a snail,
Feeling blue, she wanted to just sleep again.

Tuesday brought realisation with it,
With the work and the week not allowing her
to sit,
With chores piling up and the weekend far
away,
Feeling grumpy, she kept her feelings at bay.

Wednesday came like a confused kid,
With joys of its own and mischief that it hid,
The day seemed calm and the weather fine,
Feeling bored, she looked at the sky with a
smile.

Thursday had the charm of a new lover,
With good times ahead and the tiring ones
over,

All around were the beings all quite gay,
Feeling happy, she spent the entire day.

Friday was the beginning of fun,
For the weekend began upon the setting of
the sun,
With giggles, rambles and tacos for the soul,
Feeling excited, she was all ready with her
goal.

Saturday meant a fun and slow day,
With brunches and movies and nothing more
to say,
This day was indeed worth the long wait,
Feeling relaxed, she sat there thanking her
fate.

Sunday marked the memorial time,
A day to reflect and a day to prepare your
future climb,
Like a moth to a flame the weekend did she
seek,
Feeling content, she prepared herself for the
coming week.

Garden

The crooked lane adorned its body,
With the leaves and twigs from the trees
beside,
Like a wise old soul who's awaiting samadhi,
It lay there bearing the prints of the times.

At the end of the lane was the mighty Banyan
tree,
Which housed all creatures – birds, bats and
bugs,
Like a loyal servant to his Master, one can see,
The Banyan tree beside a mansion that it now
hugs.

The once majestic home now remains,
Abandoned, alone and devoid of feelings,
Creepers and vines have conquered it with
their reins,
With none but one visitor for whom it lives.

Every week the weary old man,
Set his journey with a rosewood stick,
And trod along this way that he knew for an
entire lifespan,
With a bowl filled with flowers that he
himself would pick.

At the sight of him would the cuckoo sing a
hymn,
Alerting her friends of his punctual arrival,
Each week they looked forward to him,
Like devotees to their respected idol.

He would walk past his once merry and lively
home,
With the birds chirping by and few squirrels
following him afoot,

Past the tall coconut trees and into the sacred
garden would he roam,
The sunlight painting a marvellous picture as
he stood.

First he would stop by the Cashew tree,
And look down, with old memories still
warm at heart,
For there rest his parents, who once lived here
happy and free,
And at its lap would he place yellow bell
flowers, as a start.

Then he would walk up to the sturdy mango
tree,
And place few butterfly pea flowers there,
For there rest his infants who were called up
to heaven, all three,
So pure were they, hence never on this cruel
Earth they were.

At last beneath the grand Mayflower tree he
sat,
With a garland of jasmine flowers at hand,
For this is where they both used to chat,

While with the jasmine flowers he adorned
her hair strands.

The birds and squirrels always await this
ritual,
They love the food that he later gave them bit
by bit,
Alas! today they never got their food, which
was habitual,
For he never left the garden but became one
with it.

Hiraeth

Buds now began to sprout from the ground,
Which lay barren as a mind recovering from a
wound,
No trees or houses anywhere in sight,
She stood there teary eyed, holding herself
tight.

This barren land was once her home,
Where she and her brother used to happily
roam,
The yesteryear thrived with warm memories,
With a fake promise that it would last for
centuries.

A bright morning with their parents, they left
their house,
And returned the next day to nothing but
panic shouts,
With the dusk did the landslide attack,
Taking everything with it, all in the pitch
black.

The entire place was a clean canvas,
Where once thrived her entire life, like a
painting of happiness,
There were frantic neighbours in search of
loved ones,
And the air splitting with the cries of parents,
daughters and sons.

Nothing remained, neither a paper, brick or
dust,
She hoped it would all be a dream, Oh! it
must!
This felt like a new life where nothing
remained,
But thankful was she that her family
sustained.

Each time she comes here to stare from afar,
This place now etched in her heart like a scar,
She knew this would now always stay there,
cold,
The feeling of Hiraeth that enveloped her
soul.

Ice cream

The little girl lay down on the grass,
With her twinkling eyes closed, basking in the
sun,
She listened to the breeze, digging her tiny
hands into the moss,
She enjoyed the warmth, her hair tied in a
lazy bun.

At the sound of the mother's steps she sat up,
Her beautiful smile lighting this bright sunny
day,
She ran to her mother like an eager pup,
With the fuzzy cat at her heels all the way.

They played in the garden with the butterflies
afloat,
Picking the colourful and fragrant fallen
flowers,
She looked in awe at the petite boat,
That her mother made with her origami
powers.

She helped her mother plant new seeds,
Now a grown-up girl, all of four,
She merrily played in the mud, picking out
the weeds,
When that enchanting music came up, as
yesterday and the day before.

The bells played her favourite music from
school,
And she crept up the fence with curious eyes
searching the source,
Her mother said that she would take her to it
soon,
As a reward for helping with her tiny hands
across.

In came the music truck and out popped a
man,
Who gave her a cone with a cloud she saw in
the sky,
She dug her mouth into it after a quick scan,
It was exactly how she imagined the cloud up
high.

The cool ecstasy melted in her mouth like
magic,
She thanked the man who brought her the
clouds,
Now this was a memory years later she would
recall, nostalgic,
The ice cream man who brought her favourite
clouds to the grounds.

Joy

The taunts and giggles resumed when we met,
Time washed away by the wave of emotions
that set,
Though adults now, just girls we were with
one another,
Carefree of worries and laying next to each
other,
Each bathing in the warm presence of old
friends,
The little joys of our time on Earth...

Sitting in the veranda of our little nest,
Chatting lazily about nothing and everything
to our best,
We enjoyed the beautiful dusk that was born,
I looked at my parents with my worries all
gone,

We found comfort in this ritual of ours,
The little joys of our time on Earth...

We sat in our den with the lingering love to
wrap,
With his hands on my feet which lay safe on
his lap,
The comfort of mere existence playing like a
song,
Joking and bickering with each other all
along,
Both etching memories with the tiny little
things,
The little joys of our time on Earth...

The breeze danced with my lazy hair strands,
As I lay on my bed with a book in my hands,
The window brought in the gleeful sunshine,
That gave me warmth as I transcended
through time,
This here was a feeling of bliss,
The little joys of my time on Earth...

Kalon

Soot covered her age-old face,
And tiny wrinkles adorned with grace,
Proud was she to have educated her cubs,
By cleaning gardens all through the years,
Her existence reflected Kalon...

The mighty soldier sat near the river,
Looking down at his arm, he felt a winner,
At the price of his arm, could he save an
entire village,
The happiness of those people etched in his
mind's image,
His powerful eyes reflected Kalon...

The kids saved up with the scraps they had,
To buy a pair of shoes for their dad,
For months in the rain and sun did he go
barefoot,
In the thirst to give his kids a morsel of good
food,
Their love reflected Kalon...

Beauty that transcends the physical form,
Beauty that unites all energies and souls,
Beauty beyond what the eyes perceive,
Beauty beyond what the words can describe,
That reflects the essence of Kalon...

Listen

Listen to the air that you breathe each
moment,
Struggling to stay clean as you, like an
opponent,
Pollute her body, mind and soul,
The devils of pollutants devouring her in
whole,

Listen to the water that keeps you alive,
In which abundant lifeforms thrive,
Depleting which skyscrapers are built,
And waste is thrown into, with hardly any
guilt.

Listen to the soil on which you stand,
From which its lungs are stripped off on
demand,
Naked and barren lies the land there,
Not a plant or tree remains to help repair.

Listen to the cries of nature that you see,
Occurring every now and then on land or sea,
Remember this is our place to share,
Else shall you destroy yourself, with nothing
to spare.

Master

The lonely dog arrived as the sun rose,
To a bowl full of food and a warm smile, his
daily dose,
This ritual began a few years back,
When he met this old man in his tiny little
shack.

The dog ate calmly, feeling safe in the love
that he got,
The man never said a word, though his eyes
spoke a lot,
Often would the dog arrive at dusk near the
pond,
And sit at the man's heels, both staring at the
horizon and beyond.

They drank the nectar of each other's love,
In this lonely world into which they were
shoved,
The dog never knew humans had emotions
other than anger,
And so became this weary old man, his
Master.

Each night after the sunlight had gone,
Would the dog look forward to the birth of
dawn,
For his life had a meaning, a purpose now,
To love his master, an emotion he now knew
how.

One such day at dusk they both sat,
With an air of melancholy that seemed to set,
They looked teary eyed at each other,
And bade farewell with a soft stroke from his
master.

Next day came the dog with a slow trot,
But there was no master or bowl that he
could spot,

There were a few people gathered at the shack
for a while,
Beside which slept his master peacefully on
the ground, with a smile.

No

As simple as it sounds,
This word makes hearts pound,
For it brings with it emotions,
And a truckload of varied notions.

For an empath who looks at other's feelings
all the way,
This word's a torture just to say,
They think a lot about the things others
think,
And also what others think about the things
they think.

As soon as you build up the fort in your
mind,
To protect yourself from preventive forces of
all kinds,
In comes someone with a smile on their face,
And your emotional defeat you sadly
embrace.

It's okay to not want everything in life,

And to know that saying 'no' is no strife,
For pleasing all is possible for none,
And exhausting is the life that attempts this
one.

Silence can never make up for a 'no',
It needs to be expressed, this much one
should know,
For in order to see light, you need darkness
around,
It may hurt some, but it causes no harsh
wound.

Oh! twinkling stars

Oh! twinkling stars in the vast sky,
Spread like fairy dust to the eye,
Shimmering and shining all the while,
Like the eyes of an infant, so fragile.

Oh! twinkling stars, you shine through the
day,
In light your presence is void, they say,
But you store the light in your strong heart,
And shine through the dark when all hopes
depart.

Oh! twinkling stars so far and bright,
You bring happiness to anyone's sight,
I wonder how you feel up there while you fly,
Am I too a shining star far away, in your eye?

Punishment

The little boy sat in class each day,
Looking out the window as the green trees
sway,
He seemed bored with the tasks given in class,
Much to the despair of each teacher, alas!

Each day would the poor boy be punished,
Yet never did his dreams in the day diminish,
Then came a new teacher who saw him smile,
In his own world where he travelled many a
mile.

She asked him to stand outside the room,
And to note down his dreams that ever
bloomed,
Standing out was fine as he did this often,

But to write seemed a feat that he loathed
and felt awful.

With a sigh he wrote down of the kingdoms
afar,
And of creatures that roamed on a shining
star,
Of fairies that carried magic wands,
And of goblins that tricked everyone with
their hands.

At the end of an hour, he had a marvellous
story,
And to this day he remembers the teacher, for
she,
Gave him a day that had much to offer,
With a punishment that birthed a wonderful
author.

Queen of the night

When Sun goes down and the light goes away,
The Queen ascends her throne and the stars
make way,
Her celestial light enchanting the beings all
around,
She rules all night while in our dreams are we
bound.

The water on Earth glimmers in her aura,
As if caught in a trance in a milky sauna,
She plays with the shadows that everyone
fears,
And with the mighty waves that we often
hear.

Once a fortnight does she adorn a veil,
That slithers across her face as the months
sail,
Once a fortnight does she shows her entire
face,
And then stands the Earth spellbound in her
grace.

She moves across lands observing all,
Resting on her throne of clouds that heed her
call,
At the break of dawn does she retire,
The Queen of the night that all beings desire.

Rain

The first rain that arrives,
After long dry summer months,
Upon which all vegetation thrives,
And at the sign of which the fat toad jumps.

With a band of clouds and a rumble to
announce,
Arrived the drops of life upon the ground,
Out came the rain flies from their safe house,
Dancing in ecstasy with friends all around.

At the gentle touch of the drops,
Like a sweet caress from a longing lover,
Swooned the soil and the rocks,
With the fragrance of the earth spreading all
over.

Pitter-patter played the rain,
The music to which all creatures did heed,
Down poured the nectar from the clouds
again,
Providing us bliss like the heavenly mead.

Sweetmeat street

Step by step walked I into,
The magical street where life found fun,
Day by day it blossomed too,
Shining brightly under the moon or sun.

The cobbled walks had a history to tell,
Of the food that became the spine of the
land,
Of traders that came from afar to sell,
And of artists that became the pride of this
land.

The shops were beaded together as a maze,
Bustling with energy that was filled in the air,
Vibrant colours and lights adorned all ways,
The street thrived like a fair with nothing to
compare.

The delicious smell of the sweetmeats and
snacks,
Enveloped the place like a mother's embrace,
Often would you be trapped in your own
tracks,
For that was the magic of this special place.

Proud am I to call this city my home,
With ancient history well preserved all
around,
This place too wasn't built in a day, as Rome,
With the sweetmeat street, which keeps one
spellbound.

Tooth

The little girl came back from school,
Worried and scared, holding her mouth,
Trembling and wide eyed she stood up on the
stool,
And showed her mother what it was all
about.

Her tiny tooth had started to twitch,
'It will fall off' informed her wise best friend,
She thought she was turning into a witch,
And thus on her mother's face, a smile spread.

Just like a flower makes way for the fruit,
These tiny white buds make way for a strong
one,
So be a strong girl and don't stay mute,
Said her mother to her tiny bun.

At the end of the week,
Came out the naughty tooth,
Swoosh! She ran to her mother with a shriek,
Who picked her up along with the tooth.

Every night a mystic fairy comes,
Seeking a tooth to make fairy dust,
So place this beside the pillow of yours,
And you get a surprise that the fairy shall
entrust.

Saying this, her mother smiled,
And hearing this, she blinked her wide eyes,
That night the tooth lay on the pillow beside
the eager child,
And the next day was she the first to rise.

Upon her pillow, there lay no tooth,
But a shiny silver coin on a Thank You note,
This made her day and her pain did soothe,
And she cherished forever the note the fairy
wrote.

Utopia

Where the air feels clean,
And the water crystal clear,
Surrounded around by everything green,
And all lived happily with nothing to fear.

Where wars never occur,
And blood never shed,
With no one to conquer,
And peace remains instead.

Where nothing is judged,
And with nothing to hate,
With your mark never smudged,
By any jealous fate.

Where everything sustains,
And nothing is destroyed,
So that the future obtains,
What you too enjoyed.

Alas! Utopia it is!

Voice of the morning

At the crack of dawn,
Did the leaves all adorn,
The tiny pearls of dew,
That the morning mist threw.

While all life slept,
And the slivers of light crept,
Out came the morning call,
From the rooster standing tall.

He woke up each day,
And climbed up the hay,
Where he could see all,
Be it big or small.

After a long deep breath,
Would he then call at length,
To wake everyone all the way,
To this wonderful new day.

The rooster stood proud,
His voice so profound,

Yet so subtle,
That it was indeed a puzzle.

Wish of nature

Every time you look,
With each short glance that you took,
I wish you would also see,
The beauty that lies within me.

Every time that you hear,
The sounds faint or clear,
I wish you would also listen,
To the pleas of mine in addition.

Every time that you touch,
My leaves, trees or such,
I wish you would also feel,
My diminishing life that you steal.

With each step that you take,
Is my existence at stake,
I wish this manner you would drop,
For it's still not late to stop.

I wish you give me time to breathe,
I wish my gifts you never deplete,
I wish to stay for generations to come,
I wish my protector you do become.

Xanadu

Beyond the hills and above the skies,
In the gloomy days with dark winter nights,
When all hopes cease,
And the minds lose all peace.

Out appears the enchanting land,
Apparating slowly with fine magic sand,
The mystic colours of pink, green and blue,
Dancing to the patterns that the heavens
drew.

'Twas the land of all happy souls,
Where all fantastic beings stroll,
Hidden is the land in this vast sky,
Safe and away where no one shall pry.

When the magical beings cast spells,
On the stars and comets that dwell,
Can the naked eye catch a glimpse,
Of this mystic abode in a wisp.

Blessed are the ones,
Who catch a glimpse at least once,
Of this Xanadu called Aurora,
That keeps you spellbound in its aura.

Yearn

I yearn for the days,
When time stayed still,
No frown scarred the face,
And worries were nil.

To remain as a child,
Staring with curious eyes,
To run around wild,
Till my spirits rise.

With mischief at hand,
No thoughts to hold me back,
The days never bland,
And no self-doubt to stack.

The mind devoid of thoughts,
That tie down this soul,
The emotional knots,
Erased away in whole.

I yearn for those days,
I yearn for those times,
Which I shall chase,
Across my lifetimes.

Zen

What is zen?
Asked the curious disciple,
To the monk in front,
Who seemed deep in bliss.

With a serene smile,
Along with his soothing gaze,
Replied the monk,
In his gentle voice.

When the senses of your pristine body,
Sense without judgements,
Observe without comments,
And take all in with no prejudice.

When no thoughts are formed in the busy
mind,
When void forms the basic essence,
For thoughts are either past or future,
And never about the present.

When all becomes a dream, you see,
That's when you wake up again,
To the ever-existing reality,
To the reality of Zen.

9 789369 549856